RACE IN
AMERICA

WHAT ARE RACE AND RACISM?

BY SUE BRADFORD EDWARDS

CONTENT CONSULTANT
Duchess Harris, JD, PhD
Professor and Chair
American Studies Department
Macalester College

Essential Library

An Imprint of Abdo Publishing | abdopublishing.com

ABDOPUBLISHING.COM

Published by Abdo Publishing, a division of ABDO, PO Box 398166, Minneapolis, Minnesota 55439. Copyright © 2018 by Abdo Consulting Group, Inc. International copyrights reserved in all countries. No part of this book may be reproduced in any form without written permission from the publisher. Essential Library™ is a trademark and logo of Abdo Publishing.

Printed in the United States of America, North Mankato, Minnesota
042017
092017

THIS BOOK CONTAINS RECYCLED MATERIALS

Interior Photos: Mark Stehle/AP Images, 4–5, 9, 86–87; Keith Srakocic/AP Images, 11; Universal History Archive/UIG/Getty Images, 13; iStockphoto, 16–17; ullstein bild/Getty Images, 21; GraphicaArtis/Archive Photos/Getty Images, 24–25, 28–29; Hulton Archive/Getty Images, 31; The Print Collector/Print Collector/Hulton Archive/Getty Images, 34; AP Images, 37, 40–41, 52; Bettmann/Getty Images, 43; Dorothea Lange/Department of the Interior/War Relocation Authority/National Archives and Record Administration, 45; Gene Herrick/AP Images, 49; Magnus Persson/Pacific Press/LightRocket/Getty Images, 56–57; Gary W. Green/Orlando Sentinel/MCT/Tribune News Service/Getty Images, 61; Chris O'Meara/AP Images, 62; Jason Kempin/BET/Getty Images Entertainment/Getty Images, 64; Ted S. Warren/AP Images, 67; Bob Leverone/AP Images, 73; Kevin Terrell/AP Images, 74; SolStock/iStockphoto, 76; Victor J. Blue/Bloomberg/Getty Images, 84; Matt Rourke/AP Images, 89; Yong Kim/MCT/Philadelphia Daily News/Newscom, 91; Robert Cohen/St. Louis Post-Dispatch/AP Images, 94–95; Pete Souza/White House, 98–99

Editor: Arnold Ringstad
Series Designer: Maggie Villaume

PUBLISHER'S CATALOGING-IN-PUBLICATION DATA

Names: Edwards, Sue Bradford, author.
Title: What are race and racism? / by Sue Bradford Edwards.
Description: Minneapolis, MN : Abdo Publishing, 2018. | Series: Race in America |
    Includes bibliographical references and index.
Identifiers: LCCN 2016962262 | ISBN 9781532110382 (lib. bdg.) |
    ISBN 9781680788235 (ebook)
Subjects: LCSH: Race--Juvenile literature. | Racism--Juvenile literature.
Classification: DDC 305--dc23
LC record available at http://lccn.loc.gov/2016962262

CONTENTS

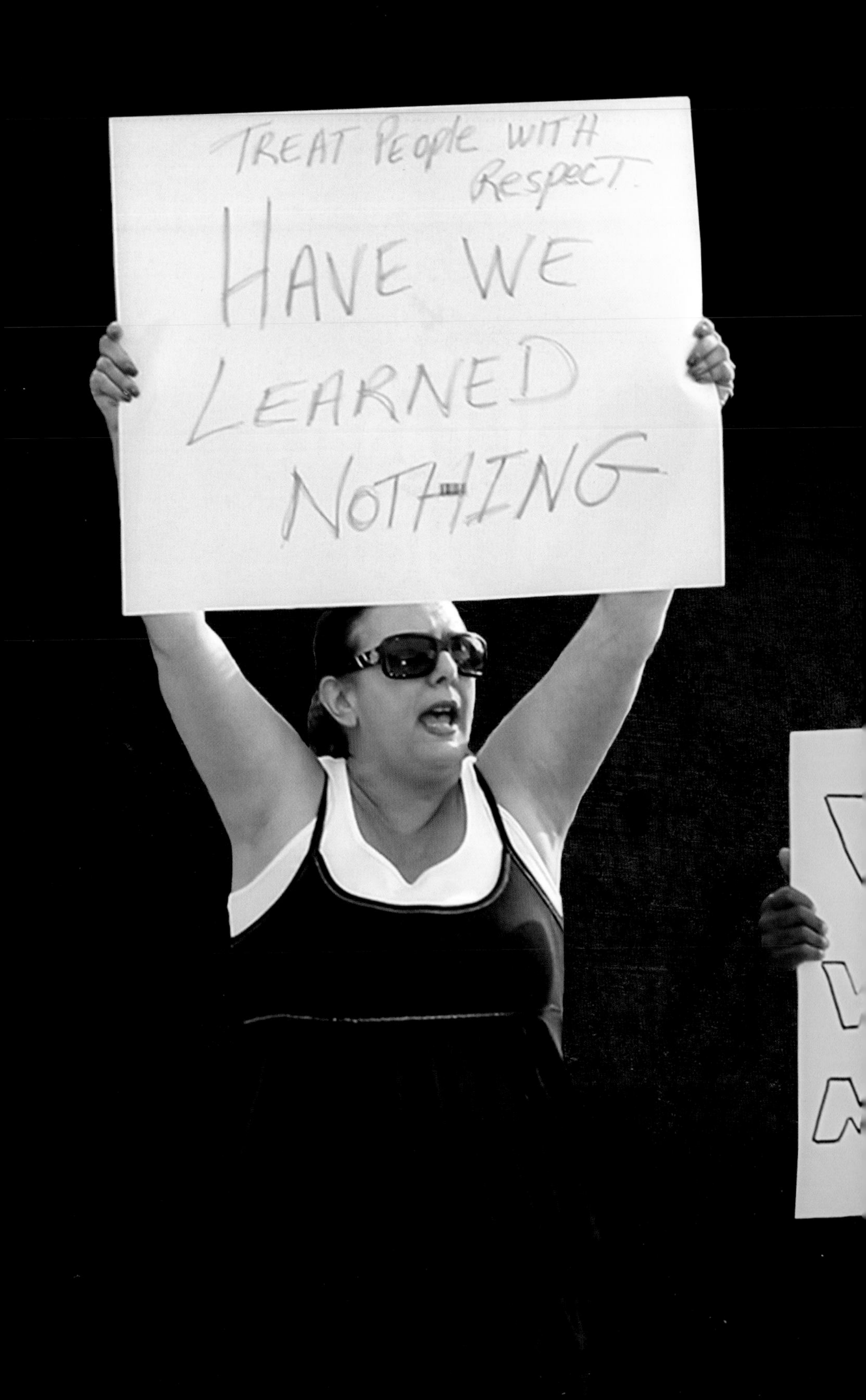
TREAT People WITH Respect.
HAVE WE LEARNED NOTHING

POOL PASSES
DENIED

When 50 children from Creative Steps Day Camp of Philadelphia, Pennsylvania, arrived at the Valley Swim Club in July 2009, they were looking forward to a day in the pool. The limited number of pools in their area meant they had few opportunities to swim. The swim club offered a solution, inviting camps like this one to rent their pool.

The swim club was located in a predominantly white area. The club's board wanted to find ways for the organization to earn more money and decided to rent the facility to local camps. By paying a fee, the camps would be able to bring children to the club once a week to swim. Alethea Wright, a black woman and the founder of Creative Steps Day Camp, had paid approximately $1,900 for the children in her care to use the club's pool. "I was excited," Wright told cable news channel CNN. "The children were excited, and parents were excited."[1]

The camp's 50 swimmers, ages eight to ten, who arrived at Valley Swim Club were African American or Hispanic. As they eagerly entered the pool, the swimmers who were already there left. These swimmers were white club members and their children. Several of the adults said things that were overheard by the camp swimmers. One woman said, "What are all of these black kids doing here?"[2] Someone else worried aloud that the black children would steal from them. Before long, a swim attendant employed by the club came out on the pool deck. This person asked the campers to leave. They did, but by this time some of the children were crying.

The next day, the swim club returned the camp's money. The club's president, John Duesler, denied race played any part in the decision. Duesler, a white man, explained the problem was that the club had simply underestimated the capacity of the pool. Because of this, he said, there weren't enough lifeguards to keep an eye on so many people. Duesler stated that asking the large group of swimmers to leave was really a matter of ensuring their safety.

WHY DON'T MORE AFRICAN AMERICAN CHILDREN SWIM?

Jeff Wiltse, a white man, is a history professor at the University of Montana. In his book *Contested Waters*, he explains that discrimination and segregation led to low rates of African American children with access to pools today. In the United States, there were two boom times for swimming. In the 1920s and 1930s, swimming first became popular as a way to exercise and have fun. In the 1950s and 1960s, many Americans fell in love with swimming as a sport.

Both of these booms left African Americans behind. Thousands of neighborhood and city pools were built in the United States. But because of segregation, African American swimmers were largely blocked from these pools. Swimming for fun did not become a part of their lives.

But that was not all Duesler had to say. He went on to explain that the large number of children who came in with the camp would change the "complexion" and "atmosphere" of the club.[3] That statement, paired with the comments overheard the day the swimmers were asked to leave, convinced many people the removal was an act of racism.

Because of this, Wright filed a lawsuit on behalf of her campers. She wanted the club to pay for the damage that had been done. Although Duesler admitted he had chosen his words poorly, he denied meaning anything racist. It would be up to the courts and the US Justice Department to determine whether or not racism had been involved. The legal process took years to complete.

RACISM DEFINED

Not everyone agrees about what is racist and what is not. Part of the problem comes from the fact that people cannot even agree about how to define the notion of race. In the United States, people often loosely define race based on the color of someone's skin. However, in the past and today, people have also applied other criteria, such as country of origin and religion.

Racism starts with the idea that each race has certain characteristics or traits that make it inherently better or

The swim club's leadership was accused of racism after ejecting the day camp students from its facility.

worse than another race. A racist person holds prejudiced views about people from other races. For instance, he or she may believe people of another race are naturally lazy or inclined to criminality. Racism often goes beyond belief to include actions. On an individual level, this may include physical violence against people due to their race. This is one example of a hate crime. On a widespread, or institutional, scale, racist actions may involve a ruling class or group passing laws that discriminate against members of a particular race.

In the United States, discussions about racism frequently center on African Americans. Since the nation's beginnings, African Americans have been victimized by a wide variety of racist systems, including slavery and discriminatory

RACE AND APPEARANCE

In some countries, defining race based on appearance can have significant career consequences. In Brazil, the government requires that 20 percent of all government jobs go to people whose ancestors came from Africa or who are mixed race.[4] Because these jobs often pay well and there is a great deal of competition for them, the government does not accept the job applicant's word about his or her race. The person has to appear before a board and answer questions about his or her family. In one region, judgments about a candidate's race are based in part on hair texture, lip size, and nose width, reinforcing racial stereotypes.

Racism in the United States is a major area of academic study.

laws. Long histories of racism have also affected other groups, including Native Americans, Asian Americans, and Latinos.

Collectively, nonwhite people are frequently described as "people of color." The term is meant to emphasize the shared experiences of unequal treatment that these people have faced and continue to face. However, not everyone who is a member of a minority group appreciates the label "people of color." They feel that many racial labels ignore their variety. Being lumped together in this way can be especially disastrous when racism turns violent. On June 19, 1982, Chinese American Vincent Chin was attacked by Ronald Ebens and Michael Nitz. The white men beat him with a baseball bat until his head split open, killing him. They thought he was Japanese, and they blamed Japanese auto manufacturers for the declining US auto industry. They were convicted of manslaughter, given two years of probation, and fined $3,000.[5] Chen's murder is a reminder that perceptions of race, scapegoating, and violence can lead to tragedy.

THE CHANGING FACE OF RACISM

The basic definition of racism is relatively simple, but the ways in which racism manifests in society have changed over time. White sociologist Augie Fleras studies race and inequality at the University of Waterloo in Ontario, Canada. He divides racism in the United States following the American Civil War (1861–1865) into three categories. He describes Racism 1.0, which was widespread in the decades following the war, as outward and obvious. It featured the idea that people of certain races needed to be kept in their place. Racism 1.0 included the laws that kept African Americans in segregated schools

Until the 1960s, legal segregation set apart separate facilities for members of different races.

and prevented them from holding certain jobs. It limited the number of Chinese immigrants who could enter the United States.

In the 1960s, new laws were passed that nullified these openly racist laws. This did not get rid of racism, but it did change it in significant ways. Racism 2.0 is subtler than Racism 1.0. In other words, it seems more accepting of minority groups. Those who practice Racism 2.0 acknowledge the successes of particular members of other races. But they may wonder aloud why more members of those races can't be like those figures.

In the 2000s, laws make it more difficult to discriminate. However, many people still hold racist

DISCUSSION STARTERS

- Based on what you have read, do you feel the actions of the Valley Swim Club's president and staff were racist? Why or why not? If you aren't certain, what additional information would you need to know to decide?

- Have you witnessed acts of racism recently? If so, do you think they were intentional?

- How do you think racism today differs from racism when your teachers were in school?

beliefs, even if they do not consciously realize it. As a result, Fleras's latest incarnation of discrimination, Racism 3.0, is even more subtle. A person might not mean to make racist statements or behave in racist ways, but it still happens. These people may not even realize they are exhibiting racism until someone points it out to them.

Understanding racism, including these subtle forms, requires studying not only how racism has changed but why it has changed. To do this, it is important to learn about the history of the notion of race itself.

MODERN RACISM

African American activist Al Sharpton wrote, "There was a time when racism in the United States was defined by the shackles of enslavement and captivity. It was the most overt and vicious form of subjugation imaginable. . . . Though racism may be less blatant now in many cases, its existence is undeniable."[6]

CHAPTER TWO

WHAT IS RACE?

On US census forms, student loan paperwork, and other official forms, Americans are asked to check a box indicating their race. This information is used to gather statistics about how many people of each race live in the United States, where they live, what jobs they hold, and more. However, since there are no standard definitions of races, the data is based largely on how a person identifies rather than on an objective reality. One person can be considered African American in one place, mixed race in another, and white someplace else.

Duana Fullwiley is a researcher who studies medical anthropology, the science of health and health care in various countries and cultures. Her experience traveling to the West African country of Senegal shows just how subjective the notion of race can be. Fullwiley lives in the United States. In the United States, people often take one look at her and consider her African American. When she travels to Senegal, she first flies to France. In France, people see her and consider her *métisse*, or "mixed." When she arrives in Senegal, she says, even children as young as two recognize her as *tubaab*, which means "white" or "European" in the Wolof language.

Nothing about Fullwiley's appearance changes as she journeys from country to country. Due to varying cultures, each group of people labels her differently. Yet people around the world often act as though the labels they choose are natural and obvious.

GENETICS

Western scientists once believed an individual's heritage could objectively and concretely determine that person's race. The discovery of genes in the 1800s seemed to provide a mechanism for this. Genes are how parents pass certain physical traits down to their children. Scientists knew genes played a part in determining hair color, eye color, and more. They assumed that people who

The US Census Bureau collects and shares information about the people living in the United States. Each person who fills out a census form is asked to indicate his or her race. A full census has been taken every ten years since 1790. Between censuses, the bureau produces estimates of how the population is growing and changing. On July 1, 2015, it estimated 321,418,820 people lived in the United States. Of these, 77.1 percent were white; 13.3 percent were black or African American; 5.6 percent were Asian; 1.2 percent were American Indian or Alaskan Natives; and 0.2 percent were Native Hawaiian or other Pacific Islanders. Hispanic, Latino, or Latina people of any race made up approximately 17.6 percent of the population.[1] The term *Hispanic* generally refers to people from Spanish-speaking nations or cultures. *Latino* and *Latina* typically refer to men and women with cultural ties to any part of Latin America. Governments and organizations sometimes define these terms in slightly varying ways. A person's race is considered separately from these labels. For instance, a person could be both black and Hispanic or both white and Hispanic.

looked different, such as people from different races, varied at the genetic level. Beyond this, they also believed these genetic differences affected more than skin color.

Some scientists began lecturing on racial purity and the dangers of interbreeding. One theory held not only that whites were the superior race, but that one particular subgroup of whites, known as the Aryans, were the best of all. These people, the theory said, had been responsible for starting civilization and naturally made the best leaders. This idea became popular with the writings of the French author Joseph-Arthur, comte de Gobineau. He wrote in the mid-1800s that a civilization would be a success only if the Aryan blood within that civilization remained pure. The Aryans, according to Gobineau, would remain in power only if they did not breed with those who looked different from them. Gobineau's theory did not gain widespread acceptance, but it later inspired Adolf Hitler's Nazi regime in Germany in the 1930s and 1940s. The Nazis used the Aryan ideology to justify their genocidal campaigns against Jews and other groups.

Work in the 1960s by Harvard University zoologist Richard Lewontin began to change scientists' perceptions of the concept of race. Lewontin used a technique called gel electrophoresis to examine proteins in human blood. He found that the proteins between two people in a single

Gobineau's Aryan theories heavily influenced later racist ideas and regimes.

An illustration from 1900 shows the arrival of Christopher Columbus in the Americas. The meeting of cultures would go on to play an important historical role in the concept of race.

Race is what scientists call a social construct. Constructs are ideas that societies recognize and agree have meaning, even when these ideas have little or no objective basis in fact. People in the United States agree on a wide variety of social constructs. The notion that certain paper or metal objects known as currency hold value is one example. The idea of what it means to be a citizen is another. The existence of different races is also largely a social construct.

Physical variations between people are clearly visible and very real. Some people do have dark skin. Others have blue eyes. Some have light hair. Often, though not always,

these things correlate with the geographic origin of a
person's ancestors. But appearance as connected to the
notion of race has been used for centuries as a means to
discriminate or harm other people. As early as the Spanish
colonization of the Americas, beginning with Christopher
Columbus's voyage in 1492, Spaniards said the Native
Americans they found were not human.

Race has also been used in the United States as a
basis on which to discriminate against specific groups
of unwanted immigrants. In the 1850s, Chinese people
immigrated to the country to work in the expanding
mining and railroad industries. When competition for

THE TRIAL OF STANDING BEAR

In 1877, the Native American Ponca Nation was moved from their Nebraska homeland to Oklahoma's Indian Territory. In Oklahoma, the Ponca didn't have enough food. Many became sick with malaria. Approximately 200 Ponca died, including the son of Chief Standing Bear.[6] Before he died, the young man asked to be buried at home in Nebraska. Standing Bear left the reservation with a group of 29 Ponca to take his son home.[7] The US Army stopped them to force them to return to Oklahoma.

Standing Bear believed his people would die in Oklahoma. A sympathetic army officer found attorneys to represent him before a judge. Standing Bear told the judge, "My hand is not the same color as yours. If I pierce it, I shall feel pain. If you pierce your hand, you too will feel pain. The blood that flows will be the same color. I am a man. The same God made us both."[8] The judge declared that as fellow human beings, the Ponca had the right to decide where to live. They could return to Nebraska. Still, Native Americans would not receive the full benefits of US citizenship until 1924.

jobs became intense, white Americans complained the Chinese workers were taking their jobs. In 1882, the US Congress passed the Chinese Exclusion Act, the first US law restricting immigration. For ten years, it suspended the immigration of people from China to the United States.

People justified discrimination based on the belief that race was more than skin color. They thought that race determined behavior and health as well. Impoverished African Americans living in crowded city neighborhoods, these people believed, didn't have higher infant mortality because they were poor. They thought the higher death rate occurred because African Americans were biologically flawed. In 1896, statistician Frederick Hoffman even predicted that these differences would lead to an African American extinction. But modern science has recognized no such differences.

Despite race's link to prejudice and racism, it is also used as a source of pride and solidarity. Black History Month focuses students' attention on African American heritage and highlights examples of outstanding African Americans who have made significant contributions to the United States. For groups who have long been victims of racial discrimination, such pride can help them stand against the racist attitudes that remain common in American society.

| DISCUSSION STARTERS |

- With what race do you identify? Why?

- Have you ever had anyone say you belonged to a race other than the one with which you identify? If so, what was your reaction to this?

- How easy or hard do you think it is to label another person's race? Why do you think this is?

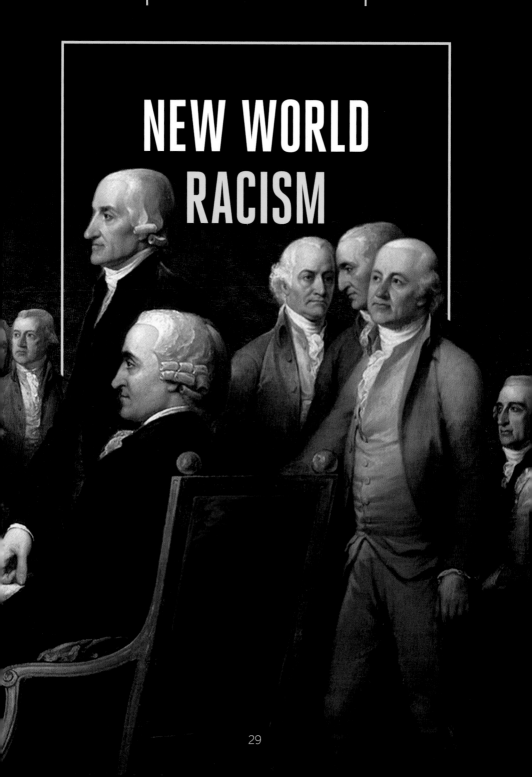

NEW WORLD
RACISM

With the Naturalization Act of 1790, the United States legally defined who could and could not be a citizen based on three requirements. First, the person had to have lived in the United States for two years. Second, someone who wanted to be a citizen had to be of good character. Third, the law limited the citizenship process to "any alien, being a free white person."[1] This part of the criteria left out African Americans, both enslaved and free, and Native Americans. It also excluded later Asian arrivals, such as the Chinese people who immigrated to California and the American West.

Starting in the 1600s, many early European immigrants in North America worked to make their fortune. The idea was not to make enough to feed a family and get by. They wanted to be rich. It did not take these immigrants long to realize the best way to do this was to farm one specific crop: tobacco.

To make a lot of money growing tobacco, farmers needed vast areas of farmland. They grew crops on enormous farms called plantations. The bigger the plantation, the more workers they needed. Some workers would have to plow and plant. Others took care of the animals that did the plowing. Workers harvested the crops and took care of the owner's home and family.

The economy of the Southern United States was built upon the cheap labor of enslaved people.

Paying the workers required to do all of this would mean sharing the wealth. Many farmers did not want to do this, so they looked for cheaper sources of labor. Indentured servants from Europe were one option. In the indentured servitude system, a plantation owner would pay for a servant's journey from Europe to North America. The servant would then owe the plantation owner labor for a set number of years. Once this time was up, the servant would be free to start his or her own farm.

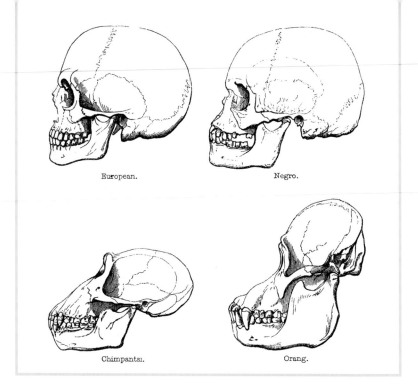

European.

Negro.

Chimpantsı.

Orang.

Diagrams produced by Morton and similar scientists suggested Europeans were significantly biologically distinct from Africans.

POST-CIVIL WAR REACTION

The American Civil War was fought in large part over the issue of slavery. Proslavery Southern states, or the Confederacy, attempted to secede from the United States. The North, or the Union, waged war to quell the rebellion. It eventually took an antislavery position. The Northern victory in 1865 reunited the nation and brought about the end of slavery in the United States.

The war freed African Americans from slavery, but their treatment was still highly unequal. People who believed whites were superior worked hard to maintain the status quo that kept whites at the top of society and others at the bottom. A variety of legislation known collectively as Jim Crow laws made segregation and unequal treatment legal in many states. The Ku Klux Klan (KKK), a terrorist group aiming to frighten, harass, and kill African Americans, was founded. And by the early 1900s, scientific racism found a new home in the emerging field of eugenics. This developing science was based on notions of white supremacy and racial purity.

JIM CROW AND THE KLAN

Discriminatory Jim Crow laws separated African Americans and whites. They segregated places such as schools, parks, and libraries. They dictated who could drink from which water fountain and where African Americans could sit on buses or trains.

People who promoted Jim Crow laws justified their actions by saying the laws provided for separate but equal services. But nothing about the situation felt equal. "Travel in the segregated South for black

"JUMP JIM CROW"

Jim Crow laws are named after a racist song-and-dance act performed by white entertainer Thomas Dartmouth Rice. In 1828, Rice imitated a black slave, putting on blackface and performing a song called "Jump Jim Crow." Singing in broken English and imitating the jumpy gait of a slave with disabilities named Jim Crow, Rice sang about slave life. His act was a hit, and soon he moved from small Louisville, Kentucky, theaters to perform in New York City.

people was humiliating," said civil rights activist Diane Nash, who worked against these laws in the 1960s. "The very fact that there were separate facilities was to say to black people and white people that blacks are so subhuman and so inferior that we could not even use the public facilities white people used."[3] African Americans who tried to work for change often faced the rage of the KKK.

The KKK was founded in 1865 in Pulaski, Tennessee, by former Confederate officer Nathan Bedford Forrest. The group claimed to be a social organization working toward "chivalry, humanity, mercy and patriotism."[4]

OTHER VICTIMS OF JIM CROW

Jim Crow laws limited who could drink from which water fountains and eat lunch in which restaurants. They also limited who could get married. The laws are best known for their treatment of African Americans, but they also affected other groups. A Nebraska law from 1911 stated: "Marriages are void when one party is a white person and the other is possessed of one-eighth or more negro, Japanese, or Chinese blood."[5]

An African American who spoke out against segregation might get a nighttime visit from members of the KKK. They would arrive at the person's home wearing hoods. Sometimes they burned crosses on people's lawns. They also burned schools, harassed politicians, and beat up or murdered those who wouldn't bend to their

KKK membership climbed into the millions in the early 1900s.

will. They did not limit their reign of terror to African Americans. They also confronted white supporters of civil rights, Roman Catholics, Jews, foreigners, and anyone else who didn't agree with their racist mind-set.

EUGENICS

Post–Civil War racism wasn't confined to the American South. Eugenics had developed in Europe and soon came to the United States. Eugenics became popular in Victorian England with the work of Sir Francis Galton.

In 1863, Galton theorized that if talented people married only other talented people, they would have talented offspring. Galton's ideas came to the United States at the same time that scientists were making early discoveries about genetics. American believers in eugenics thought that if plants and animals could be bred for certain traits, the same could and should be done for people as well.

The theory gained popularity early in the 1900s. Some whites already living in the United States believed newly arriving immigrants were inferior and would have a negative impact on American bloodlines. This worry fueled the push by eugenics supporters to improve the human species through selective breeding.

Eugenics was not a fringe science. Universities and government bodies collected index cards with information on people. Researchers used the traits recorded on the index cards to determine which families were keeping

NOT JUST A SOUTHERN THING

Although many people consider extreme racism a Southern phenomenon, such sentiments could be found throughout the United States. So-called sundown towns illustrate this fact. Sundown towns are named for the signs warning African Americans to leave before nightfall. One sign in Hawthorne, California, read: "Nigger, Don't Let The Sun Set On YOU In Hawthorne."[6] Most sundown towns were in existence from 1890 to the 1960s. They were found throughout the country and were actually more common in the Midwest than in the South.

the United States from flourishing. African Americans, Asians, Native Americans, Hispanics, Jews, Eastern Europeans, poor people, and sick people were all included in this category.

This US science caught the attention of German dictator Adolf Hitler in the 1930s. US eugenics policies helped to inspire some of his Nazi regime's own eugenics schemes. The Nazis killed people they considered inferior, impure, or defective. By the time of World War II (1939–1945), their targets included Jews, gypsies, gays, the elderly, the mentally ill, and many others. Following the Nazi defeat in 1945, the regime's genocidal use of eugenics caused the practice to fall out of popularity. The US eugenics program came to an end, though racism continued to flourish.

| DISCUSSION STARTERS |

- Why do you think people tried to use science to justify racist ideas?

- Do you think people still believe there is a link between race and how people behave?

- How do people's ideas about race shape laws?

CHAPTER FOUR

THE CIVIL RIGHTS MOVEMENT

During the 1900s, many groups and individuals worked to end racist laws in the United States. One of the first organized attempts to fight Jim Crow laws came as the nation prepared to enter World War II. The American military had to be supplied with the uniforms, jeeps, aircraft, and other equipment it would need to fight a war spanning two continents. Many of the factories and other facilities that would be providing war supplies remained segregated.

Asa Philip Randolph was an African American labor organizer. Very few labor unions allowed African American workers to join their ranks. In 1936, Randolph had organized the Brotherhood of Sleeping Car Porters to give African American workers better hours and wages. Randolph realized the war could provide African American laborers an opportunity to work as something other than janitors in the factories.

In September 1940, Randolph and several other leaders met with President Franklin Delano Roosevelt. They told the president about discrimination in the military and the defense industry. Roosevelt appeared interested in what they had to say, but his advisers feared desegregation would hurt morale among Americans opposed to the move. Randolph did not give up.

Randolph played a crucial role in advancing civil rights for African Americans during World War II.

By January 1941, Roosevelt was informed Randolph was organizing a march of 100,000 African Americans on Washington.[1] They would fill the streets. They would demand to stay in the hotels. They would try to order food at segregated restaurants that allowed only white patrons. Randolph knew his protesters would not be allowed to sleep or eat in these white establishments. He arranged for African American churches and schools to feed and house the marchers.

Roosevelt worried about the turmoil such a march would cause. On June 25, 1941, he signed Executive Order 8802. It said: "There shall be no discrimination in the employment of workers in defense industries or government because of race, creed, color, or national origin."[2] The military itself would remain segregated, but workplaces at defense contractors and in the government were to be entirely desegregated. The first step in desegregation had been taken.

ENEMY CITIZENS

Even as things were improving for African Americans, they were about to get much worse for Japanese Americans. Following the December 7, 1941, Japanese attack on Pearl Harbor, government agents raided the homes of Japanese Americans. They were looking for spies and people who sympathized with the Japanese cause.

Justice in the United States is generally said to be based on the principle of "innocent until proven guilty," but that did not hold true as the nation prepared to enter World War II. Less than two months after the Pearl Harbor attack, Roosevelt signed Executive Order 9066. It authorized the forced relocation of 110,000 people of Japanese ancestry, many of them US citizens.[3] They would be removed from their homes and confined to internment camps.

US officials rounded up Japanese American families during World War II, forcing them to gather their luggage and wear identification tags before being sent to camps.

Some proponents of the plan claimed it would keep the people safe from racist attacks. But German and Italian Americans were not rounded up when the nation declared war on Germany and Italy. With only one week to plan these moves, people sold their homes, farms, and businesses as quickly as possible. Some of them were lucky enough to find neighbors who would watch their property for the duration of the war. Many sold all they had at a loss before going to live in hastily constructed desert towns.

SEGREGATED SERVICE

Even as Japanese Americans were rounded up, African Americans found work in defense factories. They also enlisted in the segregated military. The majority of black servicemen were virtually servants, employed as cooks, quartermasters in charge of stores, or gravediggers. Relatively few were sent into combat. But those who were served with distinction. The pilots of the 332nd Fighter Group,

NATIVE AMERICAN VOTES

Starting in 1887, Native Americans could become US citizens if they did two things. They had to move off the reservations where the government had placed them, and they could no longer participate in tribal government. It was not until 1924, with the passage of the Indian Citizenship Act, that all Native Americans, regardless of where they lived, became citizens.

the renowned Tuskegee Airmen, downed more than 100 enemy aircraft and destroyed dozens of enemy train cars and ships.[4] After the war, the pilots returned to the same Jim Crow laws they had faced before. But the struggle against segregation was gaining support.

Civil rights groups such as the National Association for the Advancement of Colored People (NAACP) began filing legal challenges to these laws. By the early 1950s, lawsuits challenging segregated schools had been filed in Kansas, South Carolina, Virginia, and Delaware. The most well-known of these suits is *Brown v. Board of Education*. The lawsuit argued black and white schools were inherently unequal. A local court dismissed the lawsuit, stating that schools were equal enough. But the lawyers who had brought the suit filed an appeal. Ultimately, the case would go to the US Supreme Court.

In 1954, the chief justice of the US Supreme Court, Earl Warren, said no state could have laws that denied any person equal protection. Public education, stated Warren, was a key part of a citizen's life and the basis of a democracy. He believed any child denied a strong public education would be unlikely to succeed. The court found that even if the facilities, buildings, books, and teachers were equal, segregation made African American students feel inherently inferior, interfering with their ability to learn. The US Supreme Court ordered states to integrate their schools.

TALKING THE TALK, WALKING THE WALK

Schools weren't the only area where desegregation was needed. Transportation systems, including bus routes in Montgomery, Alabama, remained segregated. Black passengers had to sit at the back of the bus, and stops in black neighborhoods were less frequent than in white areas. In an attempt to end this segregation, in March 1954 the Women's Political Council met with Montgomery mayor W. A. Gayle. They gave him their recommendations for changes in the Montgomery bus system. The meetings were cordial, but no changes were made.

More meetings between civil rights leaders and city officials were held, but still no major changes came. Segregation policies were made clearer, but they never became fairer. Leaders watched for an opportunity to do more than ask for another meeting.

On December 1, 1955, Rosa Parks refused to give up her bus seat to a white passenger. After she was arrested and released, Martin Luther King Jr. helped organize the Montgomery Bus Boycott. For 382 days, the African American population of Montgomery refused to ride the buses.[5] Walkers were sometimes harassed and threatened. African Americans who owned cars gave people rides, but they had to be careful not to get ticketed or their cars might be confiscated.

On June 5, 1956, an Alabama court said bus segregation was unconstitutional and had to end. The city bus company appealed the ruling, so the boycott continued. On November 13, the US Supreme Court struck down all laws racially segregating buses.

Rosa Parks is processed following her arrest for protesting racist segregation laws.

CLAUDETTE COLVIN

Before Rosa Parks, there was Claudette Colvin. On March 2, 1955, Colvin refused to give up her seat on a Montgomery bus. Colvin was only 16 years old. She was on her way home from school when the bus driver told her to give up her seat to a white passenger. Colvin refused, saying, "It's my constitutional right to sit here as much as that lady. I paid my fare, it's my constitutional right."[6]

Police arrested Colvin. She sat in jail for several hours before her family bailed her out. At home, the whole family stayed up all night, worried about retaliation.

The NAACP considered using Colvin's case to challenge the segregation laws. But Colvin was only a teenager. She was also pregnant. The organization felt she would attract too much negative attention. Colvin was convicted and given probation. In 1956, when two attorneys filed a lawsuit on behalf of four women who had suffered under segregated bus rules, Colvin became a part of that lawsuit. In *Browder v. Gayle*, the US Supreme Court ruled Montgomery's segregated buses were unconstitutional.

On December 21, the day after the Supreme Court's orders were delivered to city hall, Montgomery buses were desegregated. The boycott ended, but other protests continued.

On May 4, 1961, 13 activists began a bus trip from Washington, DC, through the South. The group of African Americans and whites, known as the Freedom Riders, ignored segregation laws. The African American riders used white restrooms and sat at white lunch counters. White riders used African American restrooms and lunch counters. In Anniston, Alabama, 200 angry whites surrounded the bus, throwing a bomb inside.[7] The riders escaped the bus, but the US government had to bring in federal marshals when local police ignored the violence. The Freedom Riders drew massive attention to their cause.

THE CIVIL RIGHTS ACT

As protests drew attention to the civil rights cause, public opinion slowly shifted. In June 1963, President John F. Kennedy proposed a sweeping piece of civil rights legislation. He said the United States "will not be fully free until all of its citizens are free."[8] An assassin killed Kennedy in November 1963, and the new president, Lyndon B. Johnson, signed the Civil Rights Act of 1964 into law on July 2, 1964.

The act ended segregation on the grounds of race, religion, or national origin in public places. This included restaurants, parks, theaters, courthouses,

KENNEDY'S ANNOUNCEMENT

On June 11, 1963, President John F. Kennedy addressed the nation. He had sent National Guard troops to accompany the first African American students to attend the University of Mississippi and the University of Alabama. Kennedy announced he would be sending civil rights legislation to Congress. "It ought to be possible, in short, for every American to enjoy the privileges of being American without regard to his race or his color. . . . The heart of the question is whether all Americans are to be afforded equal rights and equal opportunities."[9]

Johnson signed the Civil Rights Act of 1964 in the East Room of the White House.

and hotels. African Americans, Native Americans, and others could no longer be denied service based on race. The act also forbade job discrimination based on race, religion, gender, or national origin. Last, but not least, the act declared that no program that used federal money could discriminate.

Congress worried the Civil Rights Act was not enough, and it soon passed the Voting Rights Act of 1965. Signed by President Johnson on August 6, 1965, this law overcame legal barriers to black voters at the state and local levels. No longer would African Americans have to pass unfair tests in order to vote. Polling places would no longer be able to falsely tell African American voters they had come at the wrong day or time.

AFTER THE CIVIL RIGHTS ACT

As much as the Civil Rights Act helped, it did not cover everything. Public places can no longer discriminate, but private clubs can. There are also size limits in terms of the law's application to housing and businesses. Businesses with 15 or fewer employees remain exempt from proving they do not discriminate. So do boardinghouses and apartment buildings with three or fewer units.[10] By the 2010s, businesses with 15 or fewer workers employed 16 percent of the US labor force, or approximately 19 million people. The exemptions in housing affected 20 percent of the housing market.[11]

The Civil Rights Act created legal changes, but it could not force people to change their ideas. Republican Richard Nixon ran against Democrat Hubert Humphrey for president in 1968. White conservative voters in Southern

THE CIVIL RIGHTS ACT BY THE NUMBERS

When the 1964 Civil Rights Act finally came up for a vote in the US Senate, senators who opposed the bill tried to block any discussion. West Virginia's Senator Robert C. Byrd spoke against the bill for 14 hours and 13 minutes. This technique is known as a filibuster. It is used to impede the progress of a bill and stop it from being put to a vote. When his fellow senators were able to vote, they first voted to end the filibuster, 71 to 29. This allowed supporters of the bill to speak. When the bill came up for a vote, it passed 73 to 27 in the Senate. The House also passed the bill with a vote of 290 to 130.[12]

states had a history of voting for Democrats. To get the Southern vote, Nixon promised he would not aggressively support civil rights. Many historians believe Nixon's strategy helped him win the 1968 election.

This Southern strategy was not the only backlash against civil rights. Whites couldn't keep their schools from being desegregated, but they could move. Some white homeowners sold their homes and moved to the suburbs. This movement out of recently desegregated areas came to be known as white flight.

Another problem came as minorities who could afford to buy homes found their efforts thwarted by a practice called redlining. Redlining started in the 1930s when the Home Owners' Loan Corporation, a federal government agency, created maps of communities throughout the

United States. The maps were color-coded depending on the racial makeup of each neighborhood. Many neighborhoods with high minority populations were outlined in red. People living in these areas were unable to get mortgage loans from banks.

Although redlining is illegal, it still happens. As recently as 2015, Associated Bank was found to have denied loans to qualified applicants in minority neighborhoods in Chicago, Illinois; Milwaukee, Wisconsin; and Minneapolis, Minnesota. The US Department of Housing and Urban Development ordered the bank to make $200 million in home loans in these areas.[13] It also had to open new offices in minority neighborhoods. The laws and courts are still working to limit and end racist practices.

| DISCUSSION STARTERS |

- What arguments would you use against segregation?
- Why do you think discussions such as the initial talks between Randolph and Roosevelt sometimes fail to bring about change?
- What laws would you propose to work against racism?

CHAPTER FIVE

STRUCTURAL RACISM

year, the white rate was 5 percent and the black rate was 9.9 percent.[3]

Employment affects income, and inequality persists there as well. Household income is a measure of how much each household or family makes. In August 2014, the median white household income was $59,754. The median black income for the same month was $35,416, just 59 percent of the white figure.[4] In 1967, the median black household income was 55.3 percent of the median white household income.[5]

UNEQUAL REPRESENTATION

Minorities have unequal access not only to good jobs, but also to government representation. In 2015, there were 46 African Americans, 32 Hispanics, 11 Asians, and 2 Native Americans in the US Congress. They made up 17 percent of all members of Congress. However, these same groups represent 38 percent of the US population.[6]

THE BLACK LIVES MATTER MOVEMENT

An event in early 2012 became the flash point for a national discussion on structural racism. On the rainy evening of February 26, 2012, black teen Trayvon Martin was walking back to his father's fiancée's house as he talked on the phone with a friend. He had been to a local store to buy snacks and was returning to the house at Retreat at Twin Lakes, a gated community in

Sanford, Florida. He was spotted by local resident George Zimmerman. Zimmerman is a man with German and Peruvian ancestry who identifies his race as Hispanic on government forms. He was a member of a neighborhood watch group who patrolled the area so he could report potential crimes to the police. When he saw Martin, he immediately became suspicious of the hoodie-wearing teen and called 911. The dispatcher told Zimmerman to remain in his car, but Zimmerman decided to follow Martin. Martin spotted Zimmerman and said something to his friend on the phone. She was frightened for Martin and listened as Martin asked Zimmerman what was going

The shooting of Trayvon Martin became a focal point for activists concerned about the deadly effects of racism.

on. Then the call disconnected. Several moments later, a struggle broke out. A shot was fired, and Martin lay dead on the ground.

Initially, the police didn't file any charges against Zimmerman. He claimed he was attacked and had to

Reactions to Martin's shooting involved not only anger but also grief.

fight back. There were no witnesses to support or deny his version of events. The police had no plans to make an arrest.

Martin's family was unwilling to accept this. On March 22, his parents posted a petition on Change.org. In it, they asked people to demand Zimmerman be arrested and tried. More than 2.25 million people signed the petition.[7] As people found out about the case, they got angry. One month after Martin's death, students in 34 Miami schools walked out of class, demanding justice.[8] There was also a protest in Sanford, where the shooting took place.

On April 11, Zimmerman was arrested and charged with second-degree murder. Zimmerman's testimony didn't seem to add up. He said he had been on the ground with Martin sitting on his chest and with Martin's knees in Zimmerman's armpits. He also testified that his gun was holstered and visible. Earlier he had shown police how the gun was holstered in the small of his back. It couldn't be there and still be visible to someone sitting on his chest. Yet on July 13, 2013, the jury acquitted Zimmerman of all charges.

Public opinion following the acquittal was vocal but varied. A poll taken by ABC News and the *Washington Post* showed 86 percent of the African Americans who

Patrisse Cullors has spoken to audiences around the world about the power of activism.

responded were unhappy with the verdict. Many African Americans thought Martin would still be alive if he had not been black. Only 30 percent of whites objected to Zimmerman's acquittal.[9] Most were willing to accept Zimmerman's portrayal of Martin as argumentative and frightening.

Many African Americans believed the system worked against Martin. They expressed their outrage on Facebook and Twitter. Activist Patrisse Cullors started using the hashtag #Blacklivesmatter to express the idea that the victims of such incidents are people whose lives matter. Under the guidance of Cullors, Alicia Garza, and Opal Tometi, Black Lives Matter became an organization working to end the killings of African Americans and to change laws to bring equal justice to everyone. Such legal changes are aimed at breaking down the structural racism in US society.

| DISCUSSION STARTERS |

- What examples of white privilege have you seen or experienced?

- What are some ways to fight structural racism?

CHAPTER SIX

SILENCING VOICES

emphasize the importance of all human lives. The problem is that by emphasizing everyone, they are de-emphasizing a historically silenced group that is trying to be heard. In doing this, they are denying the importance of protests against violent racism even if that is not what they are intending to do.

Another example of people seeking to control the words and actions of protesters occurred in the summer of 2016. On Friday, August 26, quarterback Colin Kaepernick of the San Francisco, California, 49ers, took a knee when the national anthem was played before a football game, rather than standing and facing the US flag. "I am not going to stand up to show pride in a flag for a country that oppresses black people and people of color," Kaepernick told the press after the game. "To me, this is bigger than football and it would be selfish on my part to look the other way. There are bodies in the street and people getting paid leave and getting away with murder."[9] Kaepernick was speaking about African Americans and other people of color who were shot by the police.

Many people didn't think about the validity of his protest, instead criticizing him for what they saw as disrespect for the flag. A backlash against him spread rapidly. People questioned his patriotism. One of these people was Kaepernick's former teammate Alex Boone.

Some football fans spoke out against Kaepernick's protest.

Some fans criticized Kaepernick's protest, but others supported him.

"It's hard for me, because my brother was a Marine, and he lost a lot of friends over there," said Boone. "That flag obviously gives [Kaepernick] the right to do whatever he wants. I understand it. At the same time, you should have some [expletive] respect for people who served, especially people that lost their life to protect our freedom."[10] Anti-Kaepernick memes appeared on Facebook. Owners of other football teams told NFL officials that if Kaepernick was released from his 49ers contract they would not sign him.

The 49ers supported Kaepernick's right to exercise his freedom of speech. "In respecting such American principles as freedom of religion and freedom of expression, we recognize the right of an individual to choose and participate, or not, in our celebration of the national anthem."[11]

| DISCUSSION STARTERS |

- Have you heard, seen, or experienced micro-aggressions?

- What additional examples of micro-aggressions can you think of that were not listed in this chapter?

- What have you noticed more of—overt racism or micro-aggressions?

CHAPTER SEVEN

INTERNALIZED RACISM

Sometimes racist beliefs are expressed in an obvious, overt way. Victims of such racism may hear someone yell a racist comment. They may see movies with stereotypical portrayals of African Americans as gangsters, Hispanics as drug dealers, Asians as brainy nerds, or Native Americans as alcoholics.

Other times the racism they experience is covert and takes the form of a micro-aggression. One example might be a teacher who is surprised when an African American student speaks grammatically correct English. Another might be when a peer is shocked that a Chinese American student would rather play basketball than study.

When people are the victims of micro-aggressions, they may wonder if they imagined what happened. They may think they misunderstood what was

NOT FOR ME

African American film director Andre Lee said, "If I saw someone who was successful, or a family or a person who had money, I never, I never imagined I could really have it. I didn't honestly believe that I could reach the same level . . . because I would go home and we were struggling."[1] Like many young African Americans, Lee internalized the negative implications of being poor and African American. Success and happiness were for other people, not people like him.

said. Part of the problem is that micro-aggressions can be very subtle.

Constant exposure to these varying types of racism means that, at some level, people who belong to racial minorities may come to accept racist beliefs. They may not realize it has happened, but they have internalized the racism. This internalized racism can come out in unexpected, destructive ways.

DRAWING ON THE HATRED

One common way internalized racism comes out is in self-hatred. People who internalize racist beliefs may learn to dislike themselves. They may believe success in school or in a career is impossible. They might go through life thinking that ending up in prison is inevitable. Because of these ideas, they might not bother working to do well in school. They may not take steps to stay out of trouble. As a result, they never have a chance to excel. They see only repression and racism they cannot control or overcome.

For some people, internalized racism means rejecting their own culture. They do not believe their culture is as good as white American culture. Some may reject their parents' language. Many Hispanic Americans can speak some Spanish. But they may be careful about who is around when they do this. They may not want to reveal too much about their family's culture. Internalized racism may cause people to turn from their own heritage.

EFFECTS OF INTERNALIZED RACISM

Internalized racism can cause conflict within groups striving for solidarity. A researcher observed an example of this at the California Western School of Law in San Diego, California. A group of law students were members of La Raza, a Latino advocacy group. They refused to elect a blonde student to their leadership board. It wasn't that her grades were bad. Because she was blonde, she was seen as not Mexican enough to represent the group. The group rejected her candidacy even though she had been born in Mexico, spoke better Spanish than most of those who refused to vote for her, and was a well-known activist.

The same researcher saw something similar happen within La Raza Lawyers of San Diego. This group also works to support Latinos. It is composed of those who have already graduated from law school and are practicing law. When the group debated some issues, some group members would refuse to listen to other group members whom they considered too light, or too white, to have a valid opinion. With other issues, a person might be declared too dark, or not white enough, to have anything to say on the topic. This self-defeating attitude rejected some Latinos as too white and others as not white enough. It kept everyone involved from working well together.

Internalized racism can also take the form of supporting or believing negative stereotypes about other members of the group. One researcher found Latinos are often willing to buy into the idea that illegal immigrants, most commonly assumed to be Hispanic, are a drain on social services. The idea went that these people received food stamps, housing allowances, and health care without paying the taxes that support these

RACISM AND HEALTH

In 2010, University of Maryland researcher David Chae and his team gathered 95 African American men in San Francisco. The researchers measured the length of the telomeres found on the men's white blood cells. Telomeres are repetitive sequences of DNA on the end of each chromosome. Made up of sections called base pairs, they form a protective cap on the end of the chromosome. As people age, and with illness and stress, the telomeres break down. Telomeres guard against deterioration and stop chromosomes from interfering with each other. Shortened telomeres have been linked to cancer.

People start life with roughly 8,000 base pairs per telomere. Between 50 and 100 of these typically wear down each year. In theory, two 35-year-old men should have similar numbers of base pairs in their telomeres. But researchers found that the men who had experienced high levels of racism had, on average, 140 fewer base pairs.[2] The stress caused by experiencing racism can shorten telomeres, harming a person's health.

In 2016, many of Trump's supporters agreed with their candidate's plan to build a border wall to block Mexicans from entering the United States.

Chinatown. The segment was presented as an opportunity to hear what the residents thought about recent politics. In addition to asking their opinions, Watters promoted various Asian stereotypes. He asked a street vendor if his watches were "hot," or stolen. He questioned another man about whether it was the "Year of the Dragon."[7] During the segment, producers occasionally cut to clips from kung fu movies. After an outcry, Watters tweeted, "I regret if anyone found offense," suggesting those who were offended by the segment were at fault for being offended.[8] *New Yorker* writer Jiayang Fan described her reaction to the incident:

> *Watching "Watters' World: Chinatown Edition," I am reflexively reminded of the shame I felt as a young immigrant with a tenuous grasp of the English language and American culture, whose insecurity mutated into mortification on behalf of my Chinese parents and an inexorable fear that I might remain like them, a perpetual foreigner and an inferior American doomed forever to be at the mercy of those like Watters.[9]*

| DISCUSSION STARTERS |

- Why is it easy to internalize racism even if you do not mean to do it?

- How can you become aware of internalized racism?

CHAPTER EIGHT

STILL MORE TO DO

The Pennsylvania Human Relations Commission, a government group tasked with investigating civil rights issues, looked into the case involving the Valley Swim Club and the Creative Steps Day Camp. The commission needed to decide if the civil rights of the camp members and staff had been violated. Alethea Wright of the camp felt racism had been a factor in the swimmers' removal. Swim club president John Duesler claimed the club had only the safety of inexperienced swimmers in mind when they asked the group to leave. He later explained that novice swimmers require more lifeguards to keep them safe, and the club did not have enough staff on hand.

The commission agreed with Wright, finding probable cause of discrimination. It based its decision in part on the racist comments made by club members when the camp swimmers visited the club. The other factor was that the club had previously leased out its facility to other large groups. A local plumbing company rented the pool every year for a party and brought in up to 125 people. The company's events involved larger numbers of children than the day camp's party, yet there were no complaints or rude comments from club members. This led investigators to conclude the issue with the camp children was based on race. The plumbing company's parties had included five to

In the Pennsylvania swim club incident, a swimming pool became an unlikely focal point in the nation's conversation on racism.

ten African American guests, but all 50 children from the camp were African American or Hispanic.

The commission ordered the club to pay a fine. The club's lawyer said the commission hadn't reached its decision based on the facts. He believed the findings were driven instead by media attention. Because of this, the club appealed the decision, asking another court to review the finding.

In January 2010, the US Justice Department began its own investigation. In 2012, it handed down its decision. The children who had been forced to leave and who had later been denied access to the pool were each awarded a cash settlement as victims of racial discrimination. "No one may be denied the right to use a swimming pool because of their race or the color of their skin," said Thomas E. Perez, head of the department's civil rights division.[1] The Valley Swim Club was forced to file bankruptcy and sell its assets to pay the fines and legal fees. "Our hope is that this case serves as prevention for years to come and a reminder that discrimination is illegal, and has no place in Pennsylvania," said JoAnn Edwards, executive director of the Pennsylvania Human Relations Commission.[2]

A $65,000 portion of the settlement money was set aside to fund a diversity leadership council made up of

The federal government sided with Alethea Wright, the day camp's director, who believed racism had been behind the swimming pool incident.

families from the club and the camp. This effort was designed to give children from both groups a chance to interact while having fun. Camp attorney Brian Mildenberg said, "What we hope it will do is provide an experience for these two different racial groups of children to get together and actually be kids together and learn about each other."[3] The parents from both groups hope this will help them get to know each other and reduce the chances of racist incidents, intentional or accidental, from happening in the future.

INVESTIGATING CIVIL RIGHTS VIOLATIONS

In 2014, a police shooting caused tensions to flare and brought discussions of race to the forefront of national conversations. Police officer Darren Wilson shot and killed African American teen Michael Brown in Ferguson, Missouri. A Saint Louis County grand jury announced no charges would be brought against the officer. Protests led by those who wanted Wilson to go to trial turned into riots. The US Justice Department launched a review of the situation. The federal department does not bring criminal charges in such a situation, but it concluded Wilson had not violated Brown's civil rights.

The city of Ferguson did not fare as well in the department's report. The department announced the Ferguson Police Department regularly violated the First Amendment, denying African American citizens' freedom of speech. The Ferguson police also stopped African Americans who had not committed crimes and used unreasonable force. This violated the people's Fourth Amendment rights. The police focused on fines and generating money instead of justice and safety. This meant the police and the city violated African Americans' rights to due process and equal protection. The US Justice Department believed the police and city could take steps to turn things around and restore public confidence.

Citizens realized that one of the best ways to address the racism was to get to know each other. A group of local churches formed North County Churches Uniting for Racial Harmony and Justice. The group includes 23 churches from various denominations including Catholic, Presbyterian, African Methodist Episcopal, and nondenominational. The churches span both white and black communities. The group worships together and holds an annual Dr. Martin Luther King Jr. Oratory Contest as part of a daylong series of events. It sponsors health-care screenings to fight diabetes and work for fair housing. Together the group works to make its community a just and fair place to live.

WHITE ISOLATION

A study conducted in 2013 revealed the average white American's friends and family members were 91 percent white. Only 1 percent were African American. Seventy-five percent of white Americans who responded listed no African American friends or family members.[4] Writer Hillary Crosley suggested this was why so many white Americans don't believe or understand the level of racism that exists. It is simply not a part of their daily lives. African American author Rob Smith said, "When you're a white person you can literally surround yourself with all other white people because that's what's comfortable. That's a privilege that white people have, and it's something that black people don't have."[5] He explained that most African Americans have friends who aren't African American because they live in a majority white world. The reverse does not hold true for white Americans.

A year after the shooting of Michael Brown, a crowd of peaceful protesters marched in Ferguson.

PEN OR PENCIL

Not all initiatives are locally organized. Since 2012, the National Park Service has partnered with Interested Citizens for Voter Registration to put on a program called Pen or Pencil: Writing a New History. *Pen* stands for "penitentiary," or prison, in recognition of the

school-to-prison pipeline, the idea that many young people frequently suspended in school later end up in prison. A disproportionate number of these people are minorities. *Pencil* stands for "education." One of the goals of this program is to encourage young learners to succeed in school and avoid entering the criminal justice system.

Pen or Pencil programs are often held at places of historical significance, such as the Lincoln Home National Historic Site in Springfield, Illinois. Students from nearby schools attend events at these parks and learn how past heroes, such as President Abraham Lincoln, dealt with fear, prejudice, poverty, anger, and not fitting in. Students learn what choices these people made as children and how they can make positive choices in their own lives.

Race may not exist as a neatly defined scientific concept, but it is a powerful social force in the world. It shapes how people think about themselves and each other. When the thoughts are negative, they may trigger racist actions. These actions are designed to keep one or more groups of people down. The history of racism has been shaped by the struggle for wealth and power. Throughout history, racism has resulted in enslavement, forced relocation, widespread poverty, and other forms of injustice.

Racism today is often less obvious than the racism that established plantations and sundown towns. It is usually more subtle than the racism that kept African Americans from voting and moved Japanese Americans to relocation camps. But it is still here in segregated housing, low paying jobs, crumbling infrastructure, and political rhetoric.

People are working together to reduce the impact of racism in the United States. They are working to identify racist actions, whether intentional or unintentional. Activists are teaching others about these forms of modern racism and are helping everyone, including people of color, make their experiences heard. No one expects racism to disappear overnight. But people do hope that, working together, they can continue to reduce its impact.

| DISCUSSION STARTERS |

- Why do you think it is so hard to end racism?

- Do you think mixed-race discussion groups, such as the meetings between the swim club and the day camp, can help reduce racism?

- What plans or programs would you recommend to help reduce racism?

A POSTRACIAL UNITED STATES?

When Barack Obama was elected president of the United States in 2008, some journalists suggested the United States had become a postracial society. The term was coined in a 1971 *New York Times* article about a group of Southern government officials. The article described the Southern Growth Policies Board. This interstate body was created to usher in a period of Southern growth and prosperity. Several years after the passage of the Civil Rights Act, the members of the board believed racism would soon be a thing of the past.

Both in the 1970s and today, the term is most often used to describe a situation in which people are no longer racist against African Americans. With the election of an African American president, an event that would have been hard to imagine just a few decades earlier, many Americans believed

President Obama's election was a landmark event in African American history, but racial tensions in the nation persisted during his two terms.

the electoral process was no longer racist. If Obama could be elected, the thinking went, racism must be gone.

However, it has become clear that racism still persists in US society. Multiple police killings of unarmed African American men in the 2010s highlighted what many people perceived as the institutional racism of the law enforcement system. The Black Lives Matter movement emerged in part to highlight these cases and protest for reform. By the end of Obama's presidency in 2017, few people still suggested the United States had become a postracial society.

ESSENTIAL FACTS

SIGNIFICANT EVENTS

- In the 1800s, some scientists sought to provide scientific explanations for the superiority of whites and justification for society's segregation. Their theories were later discredited.

- In the 1950s and 1960s, activism and legislation helped to end government-sanctioned racist practices, including segregation.

- The sequencing of the human genome in the early 2000s showed that neatly defined racial categories have little scientific basis.

- A July 2009 incident involving a private pool club raised questions of racial discrimination and sparked a civil rights investigation.

KEY PLAYERS

- Major figures in the civil rights movement, including Philip Randolph, Rosa Parks, and Martin Luther King Jr., fought for legal equality for African Americans.

- Researchers Francis S. Collins and Craig Venter led the projects to sequence the human genome.

- George Zimmerman shot and killed Trayvon Martin as Martin was on the way home from a store on February 26, 2012. In response to the incident, Patrisse Cullors used the hashtag #Blacklivesmatter, sparking the Black Lives Matter movement.

IMPACT ON SOCIETY

In the early United States, the concept of race was used to define who was white and who could be enslaved. Even after slavery ended following the American Civil War, race was used as the basis of discrimination in society. Jim Crow laws kept African Americans segregated from whites in unequal housing, schools, and jobs. The civil rights movement of the 1950s and 1960s helped end legally sanctioned racism. Today, people are still fighting racism on several fronts. Many activists argue institutional racism leads to police shootings of people of color. At the same time, micro-aggressions, while less overt than earlier forms of racism, continue to affect people of color.

QUOTE

"There was a time when racism in the United States was defined by the shackles of enslavement and captivity. It was the most overt and vicious form of subjugation imaginable. . . . Though racism may be less blatant now in many cases, its existence is undeniable."

—*Activist Reverend Al Sharpton*

GLOSSARY

ACQUITTED
Found not guilty of a criminal act.

BLACKFACE
Makeup applied to a performer to imitate a stereotype of a black person.

CONFISCATE
To take away or seize someone's property.

CONNOTATION
An implied or deeper meaning.

CRANIOMETRY
A discredited science that tried to prove that whites had larger brains and were smarter.

DISCRIMINATION
Unfair treatment of other people, usually because of race, age, or gender.

DNA
Deoxyribonucleic acid, the chemical that is the basis of genetics, through which various traits are passed from parent to child.

EUGENICS

A discredited science that studied how to improve human beings through selective breeding.

GENOCIDAL

Relating to the deliberate mass murder of a group of people.

SEGREGATE

To separate groups of people based on race, gender, ethnicity, or other factors.

SEPARATE BUT EQUAL

Of or having to do with the policy of racial segregation whereby black people and white people have equal facilities.

SOCIOLOGIST

A person who studies the development, structure, and functioning of human society.

STEREOTYPE

A widely held but oversimplified idea about a particular type of person or thing.

STRUCTURAL RACISM

Racism that has become a part of social structures.

UNCONSTITUTIONAL

Being inconsistent with the constitution of a state or society.

ADDITIONAL RESOURCES

SELECTED BIBLIOGRAPHY

Higginbotham, F. Michael. *Ghosts of Jim Crow: Ending Racism in Post-Racial America*. New York: New York UP, 2013. Print.

Sussman, Robert Wald. *The Myth of Race: The Troubling Persistence of an Unscientific Idea*. Cambridge, MA: Harvard UP, 2014. Print.

FURTHER READINGS

Bakshi, Kelly. *Roots of Racism*. Minneapolis, MN: Abdo, 2018. Print.

Edwards, Sue Bradford, and Duchess Harris. *Black Lives Matter*. Minneapolis, MN: Abdo, 2016. Print.

Hoose, Phillip. *Claudette Colvin: Twice toward Justice*. New York: Farrar, 2015. Print.

WEBSITES

To learn more about Race in America, visit **abdobooklinks.com**. These links are routinely monitored and updated to provide the most current information available.

FOR MORE INFORMATION

For more information on this subject, contact or visit the following organizations:

THE ANTI-DEFAMATION LEAGUE
605 Third Avenue
New York, NY 10158
212-885-7700
http://www.adl.org/about-adl/

Originally founded in 1913 to fight anti-Semitism, the Anti-Defamation League is now a leading civil rights organization working to fight all forms of bigotry and defend democratic ideals and the civil rights of all people.

THE HAMPTON INSTITUTE
PO Box 4058
Clifton Park, NY 12065
http://www.hamptoninstitution.org/

The Hampton Institute researches a wide range of social problems. The Institute also works to transform this information into practical steps toward social change.

SOURCE NOTES

CHAPTER 1. POOL PASSES DENIED

1. Khara Lewin. "PA Swim Club—Accused of Racial Discrimination—Agrees to Settlement." *CNN*. CNN, 17 Aug. 2012. Web. 10 Sept. 2016.

2. Michael F. Higginbotham. *Ghosts of Jim Crow: Ending Racism in Post-Racial America*. New York: New York UP, 2013. Print. 142.

3. Karen Araiza. "Pool Boots Kids Who Might 'Change the Complexion.'" *NBC 10*. NBC 10, 29 July 2009. Web. 18 Jan. 2017.

4. Lulu Garcia-Navarro. "For Affirmative Action, Brazil Sets Up Controversial Boards to Determine Race." *NPR News*. NPR, 29 Sept. 2016. Web. 3 Oct. 2016.

5. Frank H. Wu. "Why Vincent Chin Matters." *New York Times*. New York Times, 22 June 2012. Web. 31 Oct. 2016.

6. Al Sharpton. "Racism & Bias—Can We Pause and Be Honest with Ourselves?" *Huffington Post*. Huffington Post, 27 July 2014. Web. 18 Jan. 2017.

CHAPTER 2. WHAT IS RACE?

1. "Quick Facts/United States." *US Census Bureau*. US Census Bureau, n.d. Web. 20 Sept. 2016.

2. "Interview with Richard Lewontin." *Race: The Power of an Illusion*. PBS, 2003. Web. 18 Jan. 2017.

3. "Race in a Genetic World." *Harvard Magazine*. Harvard University, May–June 2008. Web. 18 Jan. 2017.

4. Roger Highfield. "The Limits of Gene Ancestry Tests." *Telegraph*. Telegraph, 19 Oct. 2007. Web. 20 Sept. 2016.

5. Robert Wald Sussman. "There Is No Such Thing As Race." *Newsweek*. Newsweek, 8 Nov. 2014. Web. 20 Sept. 2016.

6. Dennis J. Smith. "Trial of Standing Bear." *Encyclopedia of the Great Plains*. University of Nebraska–Lincoln, n.d. Web. 18 Jan. 2017.

7. Ibid.

8. "Standing Bear's Footsteps." *PBS*. PBS, n.d. Web. 20 Sept. 2016.

CHAPTER 3. NEW WORLD RACISM

1. Andrew Glass. "US Enacts First Immigration Law, March 26, 1790." *Politico*. Politico, 26 March 2012. Web. 18 Jan. 2017.

2. Henry Louis Gates Jr. "How Many Slaves Landed in the US?" *The African Americans: Many Rivers to Cross*. PBS, n.d. Web. 18 Jan. 2017.

3. "Jim Crow Laws." *American Experience: Freedom Riders*. PBS, 2010. Web. 18 Jan. 2017.

4. "Organization and Principles of the Ku Klux Klan, 1868." *Department of History*. University at Albany, n.d. Web. 18 Jan. 2017.

5. "Jim Crow Laws." *Separate Is Not Equal.* National Museum of American History, n.d. Web. 14 Sept. 2016.

6. Laura Wexler. "Darkness on the Edge of Town." *Washington Post.* Washington Post, 23 Oct. 2005. Web. 27 Sept. 2016.

CHAPTER 4. THE CIVIL RIGHTS MOVEMENT

1. "FDR, A. Philip Randolph, and the Desegregation of the Defense Industries." *White House Historical Association.* White House Historical Association, n.d. Web. 18 Jan. 2017.

2. Ibid.

3. Julie des Jardin. "From Citizen to Enemy: The Tragedy of Japanese Internment." *History Now.* Gilda Lehrman Institute, n.d. Web. 6 Oct. 2016.

4. "Tuskegee Airmen." *Tuskegee Airmen National Historical Museum.* Tuskegee Airmen National Historical Museum, n.d. Web. 28 Mar. 2015.

5. "Martin Luther King Jr." *Biography.* A+E Networks, n.d. Web. 18 Jan. 2017.

6. "Claudette Colvin." *Biography.* A+E Networks, n.d. Web. 29 Sept. 2016.

7. "Freedom Rides." *History.* History, n.d. Web. 18 Jan. 2017.

8. "Civil Rights Announcement, 1963." *American Experience: JFK.* PBS, 2013. Web. 18 Jan. 2017.

9. "JFK on Civil Rights." *American Experience: The Kennedys.* PBS, 2012. Web. 18 Jan. 2017.

10. F. Michael Higginbotham. *Ghosts of Jim Crow: Ending Racism in Post-Racial America.* New York: New York UP, 2013. Print. 143–144.

11. Ibid. 144.

12. Jeremy Diamond. "By the Numbers: Congress and Civil Rights." *CNN.* CNN, 24 June 2014. Web. 18 Jan. 2017.

13. Emily Badger. "Redlining: Still a Thing." *Washington Post.* Washington Post, 28 May 2015. Web. 29 Sept. 2016.

CHAPTER 5. STRUCTURAL RACISM

1. "Glossary for Understanding the Dismantling of Structural Racism." *Aspen Institute.* Aspen Institute, n.d. Web. 7 Sept. 2016.

2. "The Employment Situation, August 2016." *Bureau of Labor Statistics.* US Department of Labor, 2 Sept. 2016. Web. 18 Jan. 2017.

3. Drew Desilver. "Black Unemployment Rate Is Consistently Twice That of Whites." *Pew Research Center.* Pew Research Center, 21 Aug. 2013. Web. 18 Jan. 2017.

4. "5 Disturbing Stats on Black–White Inequality." *CNN.* CNN, 21 Aug. 2014. Web. 31 Mar. 2015.

5. Drew Desilver. "Black Income Levels Are Up, but Wealth Isn't." *Pew Research Center.* Pew Research Center, 20 Aug. 2013. Web. 31 Mar. 2015.

6. Jens Manuel Krogstad. "114th Congress Is the Most Diverse Ever." *Pew Research Center.* Pew Research Center, 12 Jan. 2015. Web. 30 Sept. 2016.

7. "Prosecute the Killer of Our Son, 17-Year-Old Trayvon Martin." *Change.org.* Change.org, n.d. Web. 18 Mar. 2015.

8. Sarah Gonzalez. "Students at 34 Miami Schools Walk Out of Class for Trayvon Martin." *NPR News.* NPR, 24 Mar. 2012. Web. 18 Mar. 2015.

9. "Reaction to George Zimmerman's Acquittal." *BBC News.* BBC, 15 July 2013. Web. 16 Mar. 2015.

CHAPTER 6. SILENCING VOICES

1. Stephen Brookfield. "Teaching Our Own Racism." *Adult Learning* 25.3 (August 2014): 91. Print.

2. Ibid. 90–91.

3. Ibid. 93.

4. Danute Rasimaviciute. "Teenagers Were Asked about Micro-aggressions They Face Daily. Their Answers Are Telling." *A-Plus*. A-Plus, 23 Feb. 2015. Web. 14 Sept. 2016.

5. Emily Deruy. "Student Diversity Is Up but Teachers Are Mostly White." *American Association of Colleges for Teacher Education*. AACTE, n.d. Web. 1 Nov. 2016.

6. Augie Fleras. "Theorizing Micro-Aggressions as Racism 3.0: Shifting the Discourse." *CES* 48.2 (2016): 7–8. Print.

7. Jim Norman. "Nearly Half of Blacks Treated Unfairly 'in Last 30 Days.'" *Gallup*. Gallup, 22 Aug. 2016. Web. 1 Nov. 2016.

8. John Woodrow Cow, Scott Clement, and Theresa Vargas. "New Poll Finds 9 in 10 Native Americans Aren't Offended by Redskins Name." *Washington Post*. Washington Post, 19 May 2016. Web. 1 Nov. 2016.

9. Steve Wyche. "Colin Kaepernick Explains Why He Sat during National Anthem." *NFL.com*. NFL.com, 28 Aug. 2016. Web. 22 Sept. 2016.

10. Carly Hoilman. "Patriotic NFL Players Show Colin Kaepernick How to Properly Honor America." *Conservative Review*. Conservative Review, 29 Aug. 2016. Web. 31 Oct. 2016.

11. Steve Wyche. "Colin Kaepernick Explains Why He Sat during National Anthem." *NFL.com*. NFL.com, 28 Aug. 2016. Web. 22 Sept. 2016.

CHAPTER 7. INTERNALIZED RACISM

1. Stacy Tisdale. "The Image Gap: The Price Many of 'Us' Pay for Growing Up Different." *Huffington Post.* Huffington Post, 6 May 2014. Web. 14 Sept. 2016.

2. Juliann Hing. "Study: In Black Men, Internalized Racism Speeds Up Aging." *Colorlines.* Colorlines, 24 Jan. 2014. Web. 14 Sept. 2016.

3. Laura M. Padilla. "Internalized Oppression and Latino/as." *Group Insights* 12.3 (Summer 2004): 18. Print.

4. Carolina Moreno. "9 Outrageous Things Donald Trump Has Said about Latinos." *Huffington Post.* Huffington Post, 31 Aug. 2015. Web. 7 Oct. 2016.

5. "Chris Rock on the Billion-Dollar Black 'Good Hair' Industry." *CNN.* CNN, 4 Nov. 2009. Web. 14 Sept. 2016.

6. "Being African: What Does Hair Have to Do with It?" *BBC News.* BBC, 22 July 2015. Web. 18 Jan. 2017.

7. "Watters' World: Chinatown Edition." *Fox News.* Fox News, 3 Oct. 2016. Web. 12 Oct. 2016.

8. Jiayang Fan. "The Bullying Anti-Asian Racism of Fox News's 'Watters' World.'" *New Yorker.* New Yorker, 6 Oct. 2016. Web. 18 Jan. 2017.

9. Ibid.

CHAPTER 8. STILL MORE TO DO

1. Khara Lewin. "PA Swim Club—Accused of Racial Discrimination—Agrees to Settlement." *CNN.* CNN, 17 Aug. 2012. Web. 10 Sept. 2016.

2. Ibid.

3. Philip Lucas. "Kids Shunned from Swim Club Awarded $1.1 Million Settlement." *Philly.com.* Philly.com, 12 Aug. 2012. Web. 23 Sept. 2016.

4. Rahel Gebreyes. "Study Shows Most White Americans Don't Have Close Black Friends." *Huffington Post.* Huffington Post, 29 Aug. 2014. Web. 14 Sept. 2016.

5. Ibid.

6. Eric Westervelt. "Measuring the Power of a Prison Education." *NPR News.* NPR, 31 July 2015. Web. 18 Jan. 2017.

INDEX

ABOUT THE
AUTHOR

Sue Bradford Edwards is a Missouri nonfiction author who writes about culture and history, including matters of race and women's history. She has written a total of nine books for Abdo Publishing, including *Black Lives Matter, Women in Science, Women in Sports,* and *Hidden Human Computers.*